Philosopher Stone
from the Lower Shenandoah

AllrOneofUs Publishing
Baltimore, Md & Huntsville, Al

Michael A. Susko

While every precaution has been taken in the preparation of this book, the publisher assumes no responsibility for errors or omissions, or for damages resulting from the use of the information contained herein.

PHILOSOPHER STONE FROM THE LOWER SHENANDOAH

First edition. June 11, 2022.

Copyright © 2022 Michael A. Susko.

ISBN: 979-8201466329

Written by Michael A. Susko.

Table of Contents

To Seekers of Meaning and Beauty.

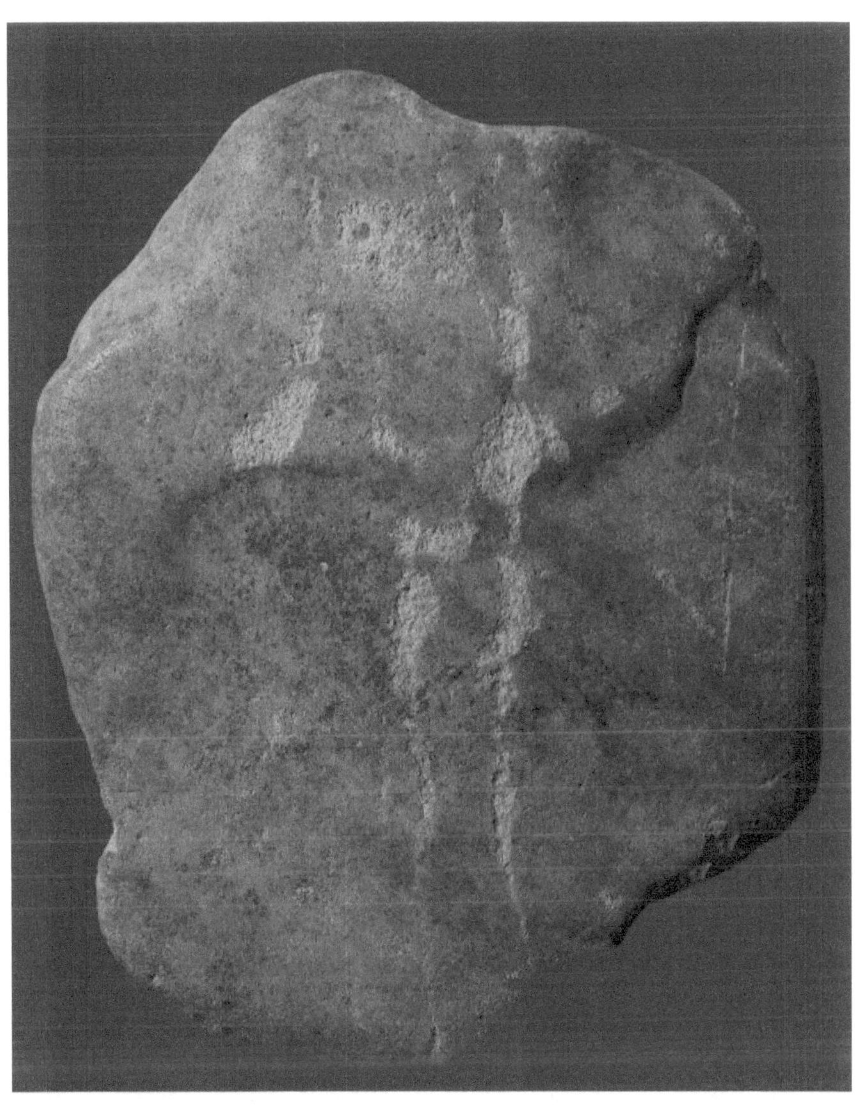

Preface

After presenting my work on the *Mystery Stone from the Shenandoah* at the Middle Atlantic Archaeological Conference this year, I talked for a lengthy period to a retired archaeologist. This professional doubts Indigenous involvement with the Stone but has been generous in engaging me with several successive emails. He suggested I write a book on the philosophic and anthropological aspects of my work, as my study raised questions to him beyond the strictly scientific. The title he suggested was *Philosopher Stone from the Lower Shenandoah.*

This journey started more than twenty years ago, when I was on a silent retreat at the Holy Cross Abbey near Berryville, Virginia. Originally from Alabama and with acres of woods beyond my immediate backyard, I liked to wander and explore. So, I ventured out of the guest house one afternoon to explore the fields and shoreline of the Shenandoah River. As I was returning, I came upon a pile of stones and picked up one with intriguing designs. The strong thought came to mind: "This is my gift to you."

I don't know who the *my* was from, but I sensed a spiritual source. At this early point, I also perceived the outlines of a human form, which looked skeletal, but I had no further idea as to its potential meaning.

I had come to this find with a symbolic attunement. For many years, I taught a course on Indigenous symbolism from around the world. In addition, I had a vision quest experience as a young adult, in which I was immersed in a symbolic realm for several weeks. Last, I have done considerable analysis of my own dreams and led groups on dream analysis. Symbols are a natural current for me, and the Stone, after detailed inspection, offered no shortage of them.

In sharing my study, I have come to realize that as persons attempt to read the stone, the Stone also reads us. Reality is a dialogical interchange. For me, the Stone served as a portal, leading me to the symbols of the Indigenous world and opening up a seemingly inexhaustible current of meaning. Even on my way to a coffee shop to start this book as I recalled the Stone, I felt my body as embedded with a skeleton, that I had gained a bone awareness from my study. To be aware of one's skeleton in a physical and spiritual sense is but one gift of this Stone. There are many, and I invite you to take a philosophic and anthropological journey of how a humble Stone can become our teacher.

Chapter One
It Isn't Even a Hypothesis

The first expert I showed the actual stone at the archaeological conference, who was familiar with Indigenous finds in the Shenandoah River, believed the markings resulted from differential wear. She had thumbed through my book Mystery Stone from the Shenandoah, which presented evidence for potential Indigenous involvement and remarked, "It isn't even a hypothesis."

I was flabbergasted, for in my understanding of science, one may raise any hypothesis. It can be disproved and shown to be false, but offering a hypothesis cannot be invalid. In a book Jules Verne raised the possibility of a journey to the center of the earth. It can now be shown to be scientifically impossible, but it was not invalid for Jules Verne to have offered this hypothesis and to have elaborated upon it.

The point of a hypothesis is to open a door. To say we can't try to open one is contrary to the first step of the scientific method. We are led to suspect there are nonscientific reasons for a summary dismissal.

In human history, persons hypothesized the earth is round, the earth rotates around the sun, that huge land masses shift on tectonic plates, and that prehistoric persons made imagery in deep caves. All of these seemed far-fetched at the time and were summarily dismissed. But the scientific method allows for such hypotheses. It also allows us, once we consider the evidence, to reject or accept the hypothesis.

So, what would be a reason for an expert to dismiss even the possibility of a hypothesis? For lack of a better word, I would suggest that experts find themselves prone to a territorial and colonial attitude. The expert, having established a workable frame for the evidence he or she has considered to date, tends to reject evidence that doesn't fit into an identified pattern. Part of this tendency for the expert to not be open to a one of a kind that is not part of a larger archaeological find.

This reminds me of photographic shoots, in which I have taken 500 to 1,000 photos. There may be one in that collection which is classic, which can be missed, if you are hasty and do not look carefully, or do not consider a view offered by another person.

In the case of stones with possible petroglyphs, experts find themselves wearied by persons presenting them with possible finds, which they tend to automatically dismiss. However, it is not every day that a person presents a find, who has taught about the symbolism of Indigenous cultures for many years, has written a 280-page book on a single stone, and presented his findings at an archaeological conference. This might invite the expert to be cautious, to ask further questions, and to read a few pages of the work. But experts are trained to doubt singular finds without context of like finds, which is no doubt heightened when the find is presented by a non-archaeologist. It is dismissed a priori, and thus the comment, "It is not even a hypothesis," is telling. But given the history of science, is it not possible that one in a hundred or a thousand of such finds are significant? Are not gems missed?

We have taken the first step in our journey. We conclude it is valid to make a hypothesis about something, particularly something studied in great detail in which considerable evidence is offered.

Without careful consideration of the evidence, a dismissal becomes more of a statement of faith, faith in our constructs, faith in our expertise, and faith that we know the boundaries of the possible.

We are ready to take a philosophic journey but also a scientific one. For philosophy is philosophy about something. In this case it is about the Stone and our philosophy as we consider this stone with markings. The nature and patterning of the markings are relevant, for they, along with the stone, are the cause for wonder that leads us on a journey.

At this point in my research, I have no overwhelming desire to convince the reader as to the origins of these markings. I can say, however, that for myself, the more I studied, the more I became convinced. But this question is but one of many the stone raises. And its value does not depend upon whether Indigenous humans purposively marked this stone hundreds of years ago. Rather, its value is that it becomes a portal to exploration and the discovery of a meaningful world view different from ours.

Chapter Two
Does the Beauty of the Stone Matter?

The Stone conveys a sense of beauty in both a visual and tactile sense. Its predominant color is brown-orange, with a coppery polished finish. Scattered white mica flakes flash when sunlight strikes them. Several dinted shapes on the stone cover some 15% of its front surface, exposing a heartstone colored white-gray and yellow, which contrasts dramatically with the brown patina.

In terms of form, the Stone possesses six softened polygonal sides, roughly paired and equal. An attractive raised wavy undulation crosses the upper third of the stone. Swathes of dark red present in an hourglass like shape intensified more in some areas, such as the oval design. The heft and size of the stone contrasts with the subtle dinted shapes. With two hands, the Stone can readily be picked up and observed, presenting its beauty to the viewer. Its tablet size and shape, paired with curious design elements, lend itself to be an object for reading and wonderment as to what story it presents.

We may ask if beauty is relevant. In many Indigenous traditions and worldwide religions, beauty reflects the sacred. The Indigenous perspective holds that the natural world is sacred. Thus, a stone which itself exhibits beauty and invites our attention is sacred. It does not need to have special markings added by human agency to achieve this status.

However, added markings by whatever means could well add to its sacred quality.

This leads us to consider what is the nature of beauty. In terms of someone who has spent hours viewing this stone, I can make an attempt. Beauty is something that holds one's attention, is pleasing to the eye and offers a strong sense of being and presence. This beauty, we will find, is connected with a mathematical sense of proportion and design. It is as if an underlying harmony of the universe is being tapped into, and sensing this, we feel a deep resonance within our own being.

Importantly, we find that Beauty is also connected with meaning or leading one to meaning. In this sense Beauty is a portal, an invitation to enter another state, one of wonderment and mystery.

That the Stone satisfies this requirement puts it in the realm of the sacred.

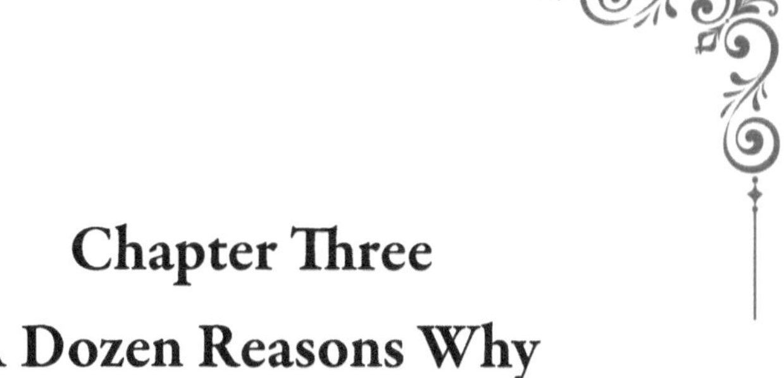

Chapter Three
A Dozen Reasons Why

The markings on the Stone remain highly relevant and pose many of the questions this study entails. In this chapter, as a preliminary, I will give a dozen reasons why it is more likely than not that intelligent agency was involved in making these markings. This serves as a summary of detailed photographic work offered in my prior work: *Mystery Stone from the Shenandoah*. Once we do this, we will go beyond the strictly scientific and consider the philosophic implications raised by the study of this Stone. Twelve plates have been provided at the end of this book to illustrate each of the reasons. They can be examined in full color detail in the book's e-book version.

1. A Mark in the Center

In the exact center of the stone, in the middle of a pelvic or butterfly like design of a plausible anthropomorph, is an indentation that has red coloring. The sacrum, a holy bone in Mesoamerica, is a portal. It is also the center of gravity in humans. This placement could be by chance, of course, but it offers a remarkable coincidence. My 13-year-old son says he can go outside and find a stone like this, and he made a cursory attempt before giving up. I suggested we would have to at least go to a stream bed to test his hypothesis. But I wonder how long would one have to search to find this combination of design? I dare say that the chances appear to be astronomical.

This find alerts us to a potential mathematical precision operative in a design. Rather than solely our aesthetic impressions, we can measure and see if there are harmonious patterns.

2. Anthropomorphic Feel and Proportion

The overall gestalt, with its array of detail, gives an impression of a human form to many. That a plough, as some experts have suggested, could create such a design is possible, but to the eye appears less likely. That a plough with centimeter wide blades could create a complex nonlinear sequence of actions at varying depths in the range of millimeters seems less likely than intelligent agency.

What of differential wear which another expert suggests? This quartz cobblestone stone is hard at the level of 7 and is able to scratch glass. I have pounded a similar stone with a steel hammer and it barely breaks the surface. My assumption would be that differential wear would have to been helped first by the surface being struck, whether by a plough, other stones in a stream, or by a human handling a hammerstone. The form of a stone in a stream gradually rounds over time and this polygonal stone was on that path. However the markings were made, they have produced elements which appear anthropomorph.

This series of elements can be measured with regards to one another. The total figure comes to an approximate human proportion of 7.5 heads, if we exclude a portion of the obviously attenuated feet lines, which could also be pointing downwards and adding to the figure's length. Interestingly too, the measures of each head approximately demarcate what is expected to be found. For example, the third head ends at the area of the navel.

Several elements thus work together to make an anthropomorphic feel and one which is skeletal. The head are, which we will consider next, has a skull-like appearance. The body continues with four torso elements: a chevron-like design, a pipe-like form, a large oval and pouch like form which presents a mystery as to their interpretation. They are disarticulated, which suggests a skeletal quality. Below that is the pelvic design, perhaps the most skeletal of all, found in the center. This is followed by semi-naturalistic leg elements, which end with attenuated feet.

Again, such proportions and correspondences point toward (but don't prove) the hypothesis of intelligent agency. At some point during an investigation, when a series of synchronicities keep manifesting, we find ourselves tipping toward a conclusion. Several signs from varying directions are often sufficient for most people to support a hypothesis as more likely than not. Humans must often must operate without waiting for absolute certitude. In judicial courts, there are levels of proof, such as in a criminal case, "Beyond a reasonable doubt" or in a civil case which only needs a "preponderance of evidence." I like the phrasing, "more likely than not," as one sufficient to point us in a fruitful direction.

In sum, the anthropomorphic feel and initial mathematical proportions allow us to offer intelligent agency as a reasonable hypothesis for being involved in this design.

3. A Head with Facial Features

Usually, a clear sign of human agency is the presence of an eyespot in the head of an anthropomorphic design. We have a clearly large one here, calling to mind that of a raptor or primate. It is deeply indented and filled with a black pigment. The head is the most complex area of the human body, and we have a similar complexity present in this head. This includes what appears to be an open mouth with beak and/or tongue, tattoo-like dark spots in the check and chin area, and radiating patterns suggestive of hair or headdress from the back of the head. If this were not enough, a second head-like oval is connected to the first by two ovular lines, and this head appears to have eye spots and mouth as well.

The head typically exhibits the personality of the figure. This squarish head in profile possesses the large eye, a mouth with beak-like extensions, and flaring designs at the back of the head, all of which create an ecstatic feel. Interestingly, the skull-like head appears to have an open mouth, which can be interpreted as talking or singing. This "singing skull" suggests a dynamic skeletal quality which is continued in the forms below.

One could again posit chance that this head shape has an eye spot and other facial elements. Yet, their presence and overall feel of the design shouts intelligent agency.

4. Plant-like Stalk with Design Elements

A parallel form to the anthropomorph's left side is a phytomorphic design. It first appears as spear-like, with a long line and a shorter angled line attached. It suggests a human signature or marking declaring that this is a worked piece. Close inspection suggests a second hypothesis, as we find plant-like extensions from this stalk. They include the angled stalk just mentioned, which has an enlarged thistle-like form at its end. On the other side, a line curls around the stone to bear a leaf like extension. Then up the stalk, at least three looping extensions end in a similar leaf-like shape. Finally, the top of the long line is crowned by a circular flower like design with petals.

A design with a straight line and arrow could have happened by chance, but what are the chances of repeated leaf-like designs topped by a petal? Again, a plausible hypothesis is that intelligent agency was involved in the making of this design.

5. Sinuous Form with a Head

Unnoticed at first, we eventually discern a natural raised, sinuous form that crosses the stone. We are ever alert to the Indigenous practice of incorporating natural curves and projections to suggest a form. So, we are not surprised to find this snake-like form has added elements which suggest a bear-like head. In particular, a natural raised area has added incisions, gouge marks and darkened spots. Capturing our immediate attention, a clear eyespot of dark pigment appears haloed by white, which may be a natural crenelation. The other eye is more indefinite, suggested by a dark spots and incisions. Importantly, the whole facial area appears highlighted by an equilateral incised triangle. Last, we note two natural projections whose ends contain a similar trefoil design are suggestive of horns. A fabulous creature is summoned by the totality of this design. And again, we hypothesize a head and body, coupled with an aesthetic sense, suggests intelligent agency.

6. A Quadruped Near the Top of the Stone

Another form that integrates into the design of the stone and pops into view once noticed is a quadruped. A clear profiled animal head with a rayed eye graces the top of the stone. The mouth appears open as if baying, and a sense of forward movement when the whole body is taken into view. The top curve of the stone forms the body naturally, and a further line suggests a rear leg, moving forward. The combination of a painted head with an eye spot combined with the natural form of the stone suggests an aesthetic capability that results from intelligent agency. As to what animal the quadruped could be, it looks like a horse at first glance. But the head could also be from the deer family, favoring an elk who have a more rectangular snout.

7. The Oval as a Center

Returning to the design in its entirety, there are central design elements, for which we now consider one. One of the largest forms which exerts a dominance in the design is an oval that is off center. It is actually at a Golden Mean proportion which creates an aesthetic dimension to this centering. A sense of center is gained by showing lines radiating from the design, which readily connects the other forms within the stone. A golden curve radiating from this point also shows a sense of connectivity to this proposed center. Interestingly, a golden mean spiral grows to include the outline of the stone itself, making for a whole.

The presence of this center with an aesthetic dimension of centering is something that is harmonious with intelligent agency.

8. Equilateral Triangles, Golden Rectangles

Complimenting the above, the designs on the stone are rife with mathematical proportions, such as equilateral triangles and golden mean rectangles. The figures mentioned above can be mapped by golden rectangles and spirals. For example, the trunk elements which form the center of the design can be readily inscribed with a golden rectangle, as well as the two heads.

While proportions can arise by chance, their repeated appearance and resultant aesthetic sense, which cumulates, argue for an increasing likelihood of intelligent agency.

9. Dints and the Angle of Striking

The presence of circular dints which often merge and are come together to make for a definite shape with clear boundaries has the look of purposive design. But a more subtle clue is t the angle of the dints on the edge of the shapes. We find one side of a shape is consistently dinted at the same angle. With the mid-torso elements of oval and chevron, we find a steep angle on the viewer's right side and a more graduated angle on the other. To my mind, this shows handedness, with a series of blows coming from a similar angle. Meanwhile, the upper leg elements show the opposite, with much steeper angles on the Viewer's left. We envision the stone was rotated, which could change the angle of percussion for different shapes. We would not expect chance strikes, or a long plough mark, to offer a consistent pattering with different shapes.

It's a subtle clue but one which is telling. And if there is evidence for handedness, we can hypothesize that an intelligent agency was involved, in this case, human.

10. Red Ochre, Red Spots and Pigment

DStretch, a software used in rock art that stresses color contrast, indicates smears of red ochre across the stone. Some of the coloring is darker around certain shapes, such as the oval. In addition, indentations toward the middle of the pelvis and the oval design are accentuated by a red spot. Last, there is a pipe-like shape which has a bright red-magenta color along its underside.

The presence of such color flourishes points toward an aesthetic and/or ritual sense, which is compatible with intelligent agency.

11. The Presence of Symbolic Resonances

The various shapes found on the Stone resonate with Indigenous symbolism of the Eastern Woodlands. Examples include plausible forms we have not described here but are documented in the longer work, such as a cross and circle design. Here I will provide two examples. The presence of beak-like shapes in the mouth area of the anthropomorph, along with a large eye, suggests associations to the bird-man, a dominant archetype with warlike associations. A second example is a subtle white outline object that looks like a dipper. The anthropomorph can be interpreted as holding this object, which holds a central place in the design. A variety of meanings are possible, and here we touch upon one. The anthropomorph is using a dipper gourd as part of a ritual action, which may be related to the shamanic theme of gift giving.

That our design has shapes readily associated with Indigenous symbolism and suggestive of ritual action is consistent with the hypothesis of intelligent agency. That accidental or random markings would compose subtle design elements that resonate with Indigenous symbols would appear to be a less likely hypothesis.

12. Designs on the Top of the Stone

As a last example, we consider a series of markings on top of the stone, most of which are connected by incised lines which lead below. Two of the designs, already mentioned, are trefoil like and lead from the incised lines from the two sides of the bear like face. (5,6 in Plate 12) A third form is present at the end of a line that goes from a rectangular form through the second head and continues to the top. Interestingly and amazingly, it ends in a hand-like design with an oval in the center (2 in Plate 12). That at least three complex designs would be present at the end of lines seem to present evidence for intelligent agency. Furthermore, the plant- like designs resonate with a flower world motif present in the Overworld, while the proposed hand with an oval call to mind the eye in hand symbol found in the Southeastern Ceremonial Complex.

Thus, to top off the stone, complex designs also show symbolic resonance. With one trefoil and the eye and hand, the design curves around the edges of the stone, as if the pattern decided to be more complex as the corner was turned. Yet again, patterning with symbolic resonance is supportive of the hypothesis of intelligent agency.

In these twelve examples, we have found various indicators for a more likely hypothesis. When we compose all of them together, the technical features with aesthetic/mathematical features with symbolic resonances, the hypothesis of intelligent agency amplifies much more. Though one may have had priori suspicion or a feeling about the design, the summation of evidence from varying directions ends up increasingly likelihood to a measure of certainty.

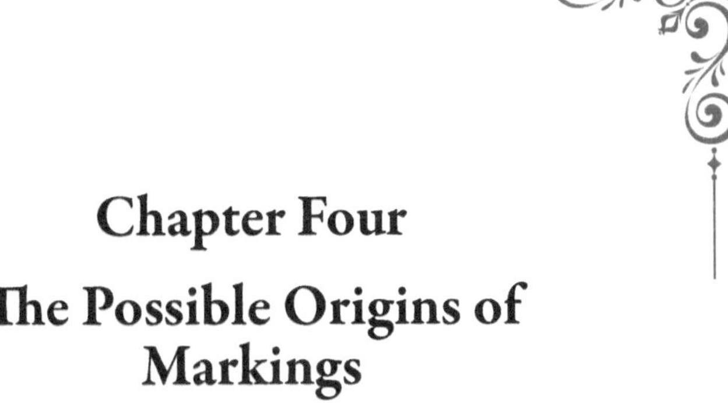

Chapter Four

The Possible Origins of Markings

The presence of markings raises the question of origins, for which we consider four main hypotheses with an added variant. As philosophers, we are open to the full range of possibilities, even if they would not be accepted or considered by scientists.

1. The markings are the result of natural processes, such as the turbidity of water.
2. They are made by accidental human markings such as plough marks.
3. They involve intentional human markings
4. They are made by sacred beings.
5. The designs are some mix of the above, such as humans adding to natural markings.

We consider each of these possibilities.

Natural Processes

We know the Stone itself was made by natural processes, of which we can list at least three: 1.) The deep earth processes which made the quartz stone. These involve the cooling of heated magma from the earth's deep interior, leftover energy from the origin of the solar system. 2.)

The impact of high turbidity of water upon the stone in a stream which served to smooth the stone's surface and round its circumference. 3.) Exposure to the elements: sun, heat, wind and rain. 4.) Colonization of its surface by biological organisms, making for a patina which altered the stone's color and texture.

While we consider these various processes as natural, we note that the Indigenous mind sees the natural world as sacred. The Western scientific vein sees the natural world as unrelated or distinct from the sacred world. Yet, if the natural world has its origins in the sacred, as western religion posits, we might expect at least a sacred resonance to be present. The Bonaventure worldview from medieval times holds that the sacred is reflected in varying degrees in the natural world.

It is an irony that the contemporary archeologists dismiss the possibility of sacred forces being involved in the natural world when the Indigenous who are being studied have such a view. In this sense a strict scientific view reveals its colonial nature, in those deep-rooted beliefs of the people it seeks to study are cursorily dismissed. I would hazard that such dismissal serves to dehumanize the Indigenous and serves to deny the rights to the Indigenous people themselves.

Science cannot render judgement on the unseen and unprovable. People report the experience of love, but science cannot prove it, as love has so many varied manifestations. Does that mean that love does not exist if science cannot prove it? One has a dream or a vision, but one cannot prove it directly. Psychology as a science accepts the presences of dreams and associates REM states with dreaming. In short, there are spheres of reality that depend on human self-report. One can have an experience nature that is like a hierophany, as when a plant is seen as on fire and as a portal to a sacred dimension. Can science say that such experiences which results in poetry and works on nature are false? The actuality is that science by itself cannot render such a judgement unless it becomes colonial and oppressive. Science is a handmaiden to the human spirit. That being said, science can establish a sphere of facts that should be respected. But these facts do not establish the totality of reality.

In my study, I am hoping to show the stone to a geologist who would be expert on cobblestones found in streams. Such an endeavor is still in process, in part because of pandemic restrictions and in part because of the scarcity of such experts. A major university in my state has a large geological department with many divisions and several dozen professors, but none have specialized in stones such as these. In ancient days stream beds, in which only hardened stones survive, were the source for stone tools, and thus were critical to the Indigenous. Today, a plethora of experts are found in the study of the inner workings of our planet and far off planets rather than the stones commonly found in stream beds.

Accidental Human Markings

Some experts examining photographs of the Stone have suggested that plough strikes were the origins of the markings. Quartz is very hard and a plough would have the force to penetrate its surface. Further, on first glance, there appear to be two long strikes across the stone, which gives the impression of a continuous strike.

I am not an expert on plough marks, and there is no large sampling on the internet or in professional publications to inform oneself. But the few examples I have seen are nowhere close to what is presented with this stone. Centimeter wide blades at regular distances will make either a continuous marking in depth and shape, or a more random buffeting leaving isolated, abstract markings.

However, the design before us is a combination of incisions, shapes of varying depths, and there are skips between the structure. If we envision two marks striking at the base of the stone, starting as incisions and becoming gouged, then stopping totally and becoming a pelvis shape design on one side, and a large oval on the other. Then up from the right side it skips outward several centimeters, makes a chevron shape, stops, makes a pipe shape, then goes on up to make three rather continuous but curved lines upward. Meanwhile, the middle contains an isolated design, faint lines leading upward, which skip and make the two ovals that are head like. On the right side, the line goes up as we've said to the oval, then skips to make a pouch like design with lines incised leading up to the top of the stone. The totality of the design does not look messy, as if the product of random buffeting, but a coherent larger gestalt.

How does our plough, which has no intelligence to guide it, and with a blunt tool of centimeter wide proportion, produce subtle discrete shapes which are in the millimeter range? In the larger work, we raised the Intelligent plough hypothesis, but it could more fittingly be described as the miraculous plough.

I will not say that the potential for a plough to make such marks is not even a hypothesis. Rather, given the evidence, it is not a likely hypothesis.

Intentional Human Markings

We have already presented a chapter on a dozen reasons the design could result from intelligent agency. The probability of it being a *human* intelligent agency seems to be made more likely by 1.) the human-like design, as any artist/marker is embodied; 2.) a human aesthetic sense of design which has mathematical expression; 3.) technical features which show that a human hand was involved; and 4.) symbolic resonances with other designs made by Indigenous humans from ancient times.

Whether or not we are convinced, the specific and detailed evidence offered from varied angles creates a serious hypothesis that is worthy of consideration. Thus, to approach the design as if it were made by humans offers a valid entry into the meaning of the Stone.

The possible presence of ancient human markings creates a feeling of awe and wonder at their presence. What is the meaning of the markings? What is the story of the human(s) who made them? How is it that I came upon such a stone? What is my responsibility and why do I feel an obligation to study the Stone and share it with the world?

With human involvement, the Stone becomes a portal to an ancient time, reaching across generations. It is a historical document, a book revealing another worldview and way of life. It presents firsthand evidence.

The Designs Are Made by Spirit Beings

The Indigenous believe that spirits can work on stones, while the scientific world would not consider this. But belief or absence of consideration is not a proof. If there is a spiritual world which can act upon this one, as major world religions believe, then it is possible that this dimension which touches humans can also touch stones. This is reflected in the story of how the major ethical principles of the Judaic-Christian tradition were inscribed on stones and given to humans.

In my experience with the Stone, I came to discover new things daily. Knowing of the Indigenous believe, I would wonder in a humorous way, what have the spirits done in the night? That the Stone is continually being worked upon and altered is another theme. We know that the patina is the work of microorganisms, so the stone itself is being subtly altering from their action. Likewise, the effect of humidity and temperature over time, even though the stone is kept inside in fairly controlled conditions, is an added factor making for change. To some extent the stone is handled and my DNA becomes part of the Stone.

But do the spirits really work on stones? The hypothesis is raised by the Indigenous worldview and not considered to be scientifically possible. But is it a valid hypothesis? Is it unprovable? What if one compares photographs over a twenty-year period and finds unexplained alterations? In theory the hypothesis could be proved, although you would have to control for changes in photographic equipment. Whether or not provable, this hypothesis opens the door to consider a spiritual world which is active in this one.

There is a variant of this hypothesis which may be more acceptable to Western minds. Perhaps it is more likely that the spirits have worked on the viewer, allowing him or her to see what was already there.

Some Combination of the Above

Some experts with whom I have shared photographs of the Stone have allowed for a combination of natural markings and ones made by humans. Thus, strike marks made by plough or other stones were further shaped, colored, and connected by incisions and selective dinting.

In this hypothesis, the Stone's beauty already held a sacred quality, which was recognized by human(s) who then added their mark. The portal present in the stone would be widened by such additions. If the stone was used in a ritual and/or meditative way, spirits could also be seen as interacting with the stone, leaving their subtle impressions.

If the world is one with a sacred energy/presence diffused throughout, then we might expect a special stone to reflect the various forces present and become imbued with a sacred quality.

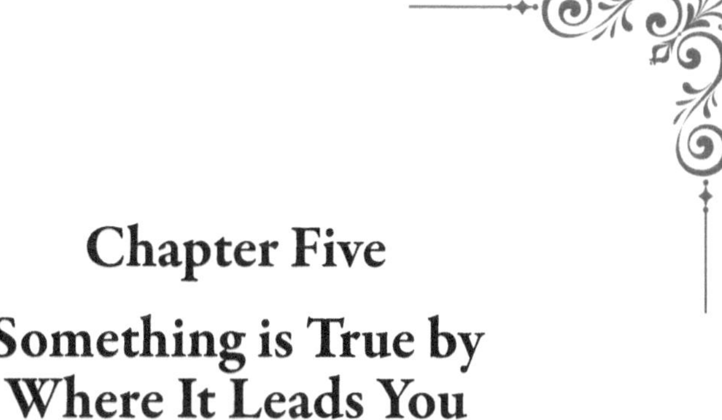

Chapter Five

Something is True by Where It Leads You

This chapter could have been entitled "The Portal Quality of the Stone." A quality of a sacred object is that opens up other dimensions and reveals things new. Thus, our Stone can be envisioned as an object that opens doors. During this study, something remarkable emerged besides the finding of designs and their symbolic associations. It was the sense of limitlessness, an unendingness, an inexhaustible sense of finding something new every time the stone was examined. A sense of the infinite is part of the quality of the sacred.

The variety of shapes that resonated with Indigenous symbols and the placement of shapes which harmonized with spatial maps used by Indigenous became a powerful incentive to study the Indigenous way. With this awareness, the question of actual Indigenous human involvement receded as a presenting issue. Rather, what became prominent was how the Stone led to greater awareness, spirituality, and a sense of wholeness.

We might reverse hypothesize and say that something which leads us to greater awareness increases the likelihood of having a rich origin. Although this is not a strict proof, it raises a paradox. A stone, with an undoubted stick figure made by Indigenous, could draw only a glance from us. Or, a stone rich in designs and full of associations, albeit of uncertain origins, could lead us on a journey. Which is of more value?

The study of the Mystery Stone opened up a variety of disciplines. In project-based learning, you take one thing and examine it from all angles. The disciplines opened up by this stone included:

1. Its geology, the questions of its origins as a stone in the deep earth and its alteration by the elements near the surface of the earth.
2. The possibility of human interaction, in which petroglyphic designs are imprinted by a variety of methods including dinting, gouging, incising, and coloring.
3. The nature of perception in terms of gestalts: what forms a gestalt, how multiple gestalts overlap, and how two dimensions interact with three dimensions.
4. The importance of light in perception, in revealing what is present. This includes the temperature of light, the angle of light, and the intensity of light.
5. Photography in which various lenses and the use of software helps to reveal what is present.
6. Its symbology, what the shapes meant to the Indigenous and how it has a universal archetypal resonance.
7. Your personal psychology interacting with the object of study. This includes awareness of your biases and your own deep interactions, including dreams about the object.

This list is not exhaustive, but it amply demonstrates the robustness of the interaction possible between this object and a person. Thus, the Stone served as a portal to various disciplines of study, inviting an interdisciplinary awareness.

The above tools are used to come to meaning, which is often perceived in tandem with beauty. But what is the meaning and beauty we are perceiving as we explore this Stone? It raises the question of what is meaning and what is beauty? We have already interpreted Beauty as a type of portal to another world. Likewise, meaning also serves as a type of resonance between the inner self and outer mystery. Meaning is something that makes our being feel good and full. It puts us at peace, not a stagnant state, but a peace which remains open and is able and confident to explore more.

The Mystery Stone has inspired several spin offs. Four Haiku and Photo books pair a Haiku with photographs of the Stone. In *Beyond the Portal*, a "fantastic voyage" has been imagined in a literary way, in which characters and shapes on the stone are encountered. The fertility of the Stone in an artistic and literary sense is important. It shows the imagination is readily engaged and meaningfully stimulated by the Stone. It is not proof or origin, but a proof of value in terms of where it leads us. Photography and 3-D surface plots have proved to be rich in the presentation of the Stone. The beauty of the stone comes out in hundreds of ways and it's routinely paired with meaning. This puts an emphatic check mark by the Stone with markings as an object that leads beyond itself.

Thus, the Stone serves as a portal to something further. It leads us somewhere. It takes us on a journey that enlarges and refreshes our being. In this sense the Stone is true.

Chapter Six
The Stone as Having Being

That the Stone may have Being seems a fantastic proposition. Yet in interacting and making discoveries with this Stone, I have found myself inclined to capitalize the word. All the summary traits, in which you become fascinated and draw multiple angles of the awareness to come to meaning and beauty work, all come together in the sense that a singular stone is still the object of our study and exploration.

A further tool can be summoned to explore this proposition. One could create or imagine a conversation with the Stone and see what results. As just mentioned, I have written a literary exploration of the Stone, imagining a journey of its characters and the encounter with various shapes. We can imagine the anthropomorph speaking, and perhaps the whole stone. What would the Stone say if it were to speak? Would it be things like, "I am totality. I embrace high and low, male and female, animal and plant?"

A stone held in one's hands is obviously not the totality of things. But a given object, especially if it has a sacred quality, can be viewed as a *microcosm* which reflects the totality or the macrocosm. We might imagine the whole universe as a Being, which has been done before. Perhaps we can, in a like vein, view the object as a microcosm, serving as a portal to larger meanings and beauty, and possessing a type of being. Can the sacred imbue objects with being, even a humble stone?

I don't know if there is Being in this stone, but I have found meaning and beauty which resonates with my being. Perhaps in the end the question serves as a useful literary and spiritual construct, rather than a scientific one, which cannot consider inanimate stones as having being. Yet this Stone, which has led us to discovery, invites us to expand the meaning of hypotheses. That is, can we make a literary or spiritual hypothesis? Are we allowed to find meaning and beauty by the use of literary tools or a spiritual modality like contemplation? If the stone leads us on a seemingly endless journey which possesses its fill of beauty and meaning, we can hypothesize that the object in question has a deep connection to being.

Does the Stone have a being itself? Maybe...

Chapter Seven

The Unending Quality of the Stone

The interaction with the Stone provided daily discoveries, reflecting the richness present. "The longer I look at it, the more I see," a participant of the Middle Atlantic Archaeological Conference told me after viewing the stone for several minutes. I had this experience over a period of weeks. The sense of unendingness, of more continuing to be revealed over time, is telling us something.

Interestingly, the Indigenous say that you see something when you are ready to see it. The Stone has its own pace of revelation. Why is this? Partly, the Stone is reading us and our ability to see. What is our being looking to see? What is it needing to see?

Perhaps this interaction of Stone and Person points to a fundamental quality of life: that reality is essentially dialogical. Much of what happens in life is two entities encountering and engaging one another, making for a type of third. For example, our immediate perception of the Stone is based on the interaction of light with its surface. When the light changes, such as its temperature as measured in Kelvin, the appearance of the Stone changes.

The main dialogical reality in this study is an interaction with the Stone. A richness in both would make for an interesting result, which reveals something about both the Stone and our being. Science wants to control, limit, or excise the contribution of our being, so we can be sure to see what is there. It is useful to make sure we see what is immediately there, but I argue it is but one step in a process. Beyond this, for example, we have to discern what future use this perception may have for us. I would venture to say that one can never eliminate the contribution of one's being in a dialogic-based reality.

Assuming we have a sense of our being and what the Stone is, we are left with a different question. What is the third reality which results from this interaction? We might say it involves feelings and an awareness that results from such interaction. In one sense, connection arises from spending considerable time with an object. In its best sense, and for want of a better word, it involves a type of love. Another feeling that could arise is repulsion, which also suggests connection, albeit one which would cause us to spend less time with the other entity.

If considerable time is spent with the Stone for its perceived richness and sense of discovery, we can hypothesize that connection, a type of love, is the third entity. If this can be true between Stone and Human, how much more is it present between human and animal, and between humans? In short, we are hypothesizing that a connecting love is at the basis of the universe.

Love can be disrupted. A stone, an animal or a human can be destroyed, and it can be done for reasons which are relatively frivolous. Such actions may involve the attempt to obtain a lesser good. With the Stone, however, a different ethical issue arises. If someone has extended interaction with an object, such as the stone and has expressed considerable "love," can that love or connection be threatened or destroyed? What if someone says that your object of attention or devotion is unworthy, and that your interaction is fanciful and false?

Rather than dismissing other people's loves, I would assert that we have an ethical obligation to be loyal to other people's loyalties. This assumes that loyalty in question is not leading one to a destructive path or causes others to be exploited. If the loyalty is born out of love and leads to a plethora and variety of meaningful explorations, then it demands respect.

Whether our constructs are scientifically provable is not the ultimate test. Rather, we ask if the interaction leads to good and bears fruit. We may disagree with the direction of the speculation, with the likelihood of a hypothesis, but it should be a respectful disagreement. Otherwise, we risk killing loves that are present in the world.

In sum, if your loyalty leads to a fruitful exploration which increases the good present in the universe, then truth is present in it.

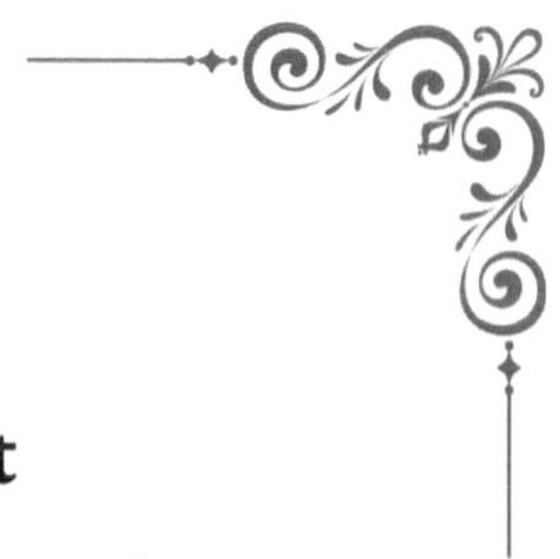

Chapter Eight
The Seemingly Banal

A person in my neighborhood, who read the *Mystery Stone* book, shared an observation. He remarked that the book showed him how something seemingly banal, as a stone found near a river, could become the object of an intensive study, a real depth dive. This points to one truth of the world, how something seemingly unimportant can present a richness. We might even say that such an object is disguised. An object may present obvious attraction and value, such as gems and precious metals. But a quartz cobblestone with some designs that once lay in the Shenandoah River is something only children, or a rock collector, may pick up. In my case, I was on a silent retreat and sensitive to the spiritual dimension. Upon picking up one stone from a pile, the strong thought came to my mind: "This is my gift to you."

In fairy tales, a young person goes on a quest that seems impossible to complete. Along the way, he or she helps someone in need, such as an elderly woman. This person, in turn, gives a gift to the youth, which enables the quest to be completed. This points to the truth that unexpected sources, often in humble guise, can become the key to accomplishing our life mission.

We might ask why is it that important clues to our path forward in life may not be obvious and disguised? Are we being tested to see if our love is expansive enough to include that which others would typically reject?

This stone with markings is disguised; its full range of design and meaning is not obvious at first sight and could be summarily and prematurely dismissed. I have thought to compare this Stone to a person. A person has much more value than any stone we can find, yet we can find ourselves dismissing persons as insignificant, as not worthy of our time. Yet that person may have the word, message, or clue that would enable us to accomplish what we are given to do. I think of a homeless person I have met, and who later came upon resources, which enabled me to complete a book project of oral histories. In this example, the poor and humble become a portal, opening a world of unexpected riches.

This leads me to reiterate a life hypothesis: The humble objects of the world can serve as a test, to see how expansive and generous our love may be. It seems as if the universe is pleased to teach us through the seemingly ordinary, more than not. Perhaps the "universe" or whatever power is embedded in it has a sense of humor, or a sense of shyness. It prefers to leave a path to the discovery rather than give you the thing outright. In short, we are given portals, often unexpectedly and which leave the work of journeying to us.

Chapter Nine

Quixotic Desire vs. the Descartes Mirror

A literary criticism article with the title similar to this chapter has stuck with me throughout the years. Basically, it made the case for the importance of desire and feeling, its pulls to action versus a cold, accurate reflection of a reality. In Cervantes' book, Don Quixote calls the conjurer the one who would only see a serving maid, not a princess, the one who would only see an old man off on a fantasy and not someone attempting to live a heroic life. While a case can certainly be made to see things as they are and take in "reflective" or factual reality, it is only a partial picture. A person may be of seemingly low stature, but through their service possess greatness. Likewise, an object can be described in all its factual detail, but the desire or impulse it awakens in us is critical as well.

What is the nature of something that awakens desire, gives rise to feelings, and causes us to act? Not everything does this and it may vary from person to person. A historical example comes to mind, in what is known as relics, a part of a body of a holy person or something that the holy person has contacted. When other believing persons view or contact this relict, feelings arise, such as a sense of devotion that moves them to become a better person. In a sense this Stone is a relic. It is a relic of the natural processes of the earth, including those of the deep earth, the turbidity of a river, and exposure to the sun. It is a relic of microorganisms forming a brown patina and making for a beautifully polished surface. Finally, it is a relic of being struck, which exposed its heartstone and left designs.

Its shape, design, and contrasts make the object attractive to our gaze and touch. When we study something at length, it can be said to be an object of devotion. Thus, the stone has taken on a sacred quality to me, and I have thought of it as similar to a monstrance, a rayed container made of gold that holds a host. In short, this Stone, in tandem with a careful examination of what is there, or the Descartes Mirror, has awakened Quixotic Desire.

This back and forth of examination of what is there to the wonder and possibility of gestalts formed, incorporates both science and imagination.

A danger of science is that it would cut off the imaginative faculty as an anthropomorphism and short circuit this second step. An overplay of imagination without careful examination of what is there in a scientific way would not be rooted in the hard nature of reality.

We are invited to a new way of seeing by the Stone. We see what is there in terms of a factual reality: shape, color, design with varying gestalts presenting, and our sense of geology and human interaction, which might reveal processes. But we are also invited to see what our being says in response to this search, the next and important step for us as humans.

We meet a person and form a first impression. But that is not all the person is, and the person we encounter is always becoming. If we are to be in touch with the fullness of life, we must allow our factual sense of reality to be complimented by imagination and our desire.

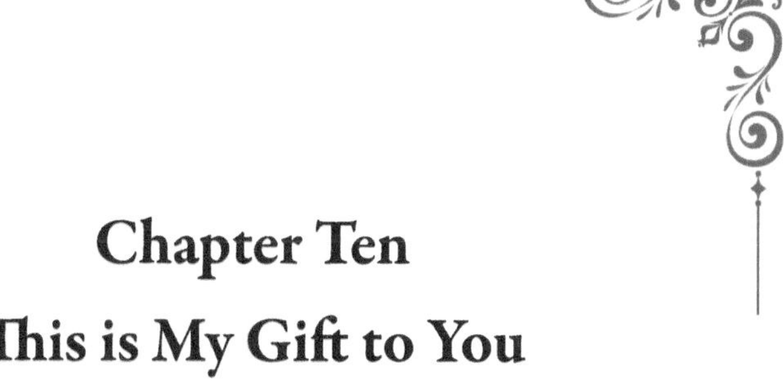

Chapter Ten
This is My Gift to You

A major impetus for this work was not only the finding of the Stone, but the message received at the time. Without this message there would not have been the directive to dedicate so much work to this Stone. While I have given some thought to the meaning of the message, I have not elaborated on its implications and the questions it raises. So, let me attempt this by asking: From where does the message come? What is the meaning of a gift? What obligation does a gift impose upon us? Why was the Stone given?

Where Does the Message Come From?

Walking back from a hike one afternoon in the fields by the Shenandoah River, I picked up a stone from a pile and the strong thought came to me: *This is my gift to you.* A question arises: where did this thought come from? William James, the foundational American psychologist, hypothesized two origins of thought. One is the production theory, in which our mind makes or produces our own thoughts. The other is the transmission theory, where our mind picks up thoughts from outside of itself. These are not mutually exclusive, with some thoughts having a more bodily origin, while others would be inspired.

At the time the thought seemed to come from outside myself. The question then can be framed: from where? Three hypotheses are offered:1) The thought comes from the land; 2) It comes from a spiritual source that is other than human, or 3) It comes from persons who once dwelt in the land and had a connection to the Stone.

The first possibility seems unlikely to our minds at first blush. How can the land gift you in a personal way? In our normal view of things, the land is not a conscious entity with a personal dimension which can offer a part of itself as "my gift." Yet something within us senses that the land and the earth are gifted to us as a whole, and that the beauty we see in nature is a wondrous gift. Thus, the land and what is found within it can be seen as a gift. But can the land give part of itself, implying it has consciousness?

We know from evolution that life was born out of the earth and mothered life. So, land or the matter contained in land must have a form of proto-consciousness. Perhaps too, as conscious beings arose and populated the land, this proto-consciousness was affected, raised and enhanced in some way. Perhaps the land as a whole with all its mix of movement and circulating features of air, wind, and water flow with a dimension of consciousness. One would have to be sensitive to this, to be tuned to the land to feel this. Can the land offer its gift in a personal way? Perhaps it can, for we can feel such.

A second possibility is that the gift comes from a spiritual source that is other than human. In Western theology this could be the triune divine being or angelic being. Such a spiritual entity sought fit to make this connection, to gift a stone to a person. By whatever name this spiritual being would go by, the entity can be seen as other, as power-filled and having a purpose in its giving. The *my* in the thought, *This is my gift to you*, was left unnamed, but its use indicates personhood and ownership of the Stone. If this thought bears any witness, the unnamed entity has the right to gift the Stone.

A third possibility is that the Stone is connected with inhabitants of the land who handled and performed work upon the Stone. This work conveyed meaning which is being passed on as a gift. As the person(s) who have done this work have passed from this world, they can gift this worked stone to another. In this entrusting, a sense of obligation is incurred, which leads us to our next question.

What is the Meaning of Gift?

We can ask what is the meaning of the *gift*. It conjures something that does not have to be given, that is freely given, that is unexpected and surprising, and perhaps also something of special value that can be treasured. Gifts are generally universally liked.

Gift speaks to a fundamental aspect of reality. Our life is a gift, something freely given to us and something of immense value. It is also something we did not ask for, although one can affirm this gift during the course of one's life. The earth we live upon is also a gift to us. We did not make the earth nor, when we are born, make the structures that exist, such as houses. Our care when we were infants, and such as it was, was gift to us. Most all of us are born into a world of gift.

One can go on, but a conclusion can be drawn that reality is full of gift. This is not to say that there is not a tragic dimension, that gifts are not taken away, or sometimes absent, such as what happens in war. But our meditation here is upon the blessing of gift. In our life we are given particular gifts. We happen to be born in a certain time and place with certain people around us, with a certain landscape. We encounter certain people, seemingly random and outside our normal family, who gift us.

In this context it is not that surprising that we might find special objects that we experience as gift. In this case, a singular quartz cobblestone became sufficiently engaging to result in extended work which demanded to be shared.

Contrary to an emphasis on gifts is earning, that we can earn and deserve things. No doubt this is part of reality too. One can take a stone and sculpt it into a shape, and that act of sculpting or work creates a type of ownership. Even here, however, the ability to work, and the innate artistic skills you have been given can be seen as part of the gifted world.

How a sense of giftedness or grace is mixed with earning things would be the start of an interesting speculation into the nature of reality. In this case, we consider a somewhat related matter: how the world of gift comes to create an obligation.

An Obligation in Receiving a Gift?

A gift by definition is freely given and there is no immediate price. However, a gift can quietly create a demand and invite a response, albeit only one voluntarily imposed. We are given a life, and that creates a demand and response that we care for our life and nurture it. We are given others, such as those who care for us when we are young, and that creates a demand and some response that the care be returned. The earth is given to us, providing air, warmth and a place to be, as well as food, and we are obligated to care for the earth in turn.

In a paradoxical way, gift obliges us to perform work. I was given this stone, but it imposed a work upon me. The work given was to carefully examine, research and make associations and gift that work back to the world. The cycle completes itself. Reality goes from gift to work, to gift again.

People may favor gifts that do not seem to impose a work, such that which is taken in as sheer entertainment. Or the "gift" may be seen as something due to the person, something already earned, without necessity for anything to be returned further. A person may inherit considerable wealth, feel it is their due, and not perceive an obligation to tithe part of that back wealth to others.

Yet, I hypothesize that the reality of gifting involves work being requested and a gifting back. Often, this is not recognized. People often fail to offer thanks for their gifts, or to show thanks by some unselfish action. Giving thanks is the start and the most elemental part of the cycle of gifting. Acknowledging the gift and giving respect to the gifter is a step in this cycle. For if we receive a gift without some acknowledgement by deed or word, without turning the gift around to spread further good, then the gift is dead ended. In the view offered here, the inherent nature of gifting and receiving gifts is to keep the energy of goodness flowing through the world. In this sense the Stone was a gift given to me, but it demanded a work and that the work be shared.

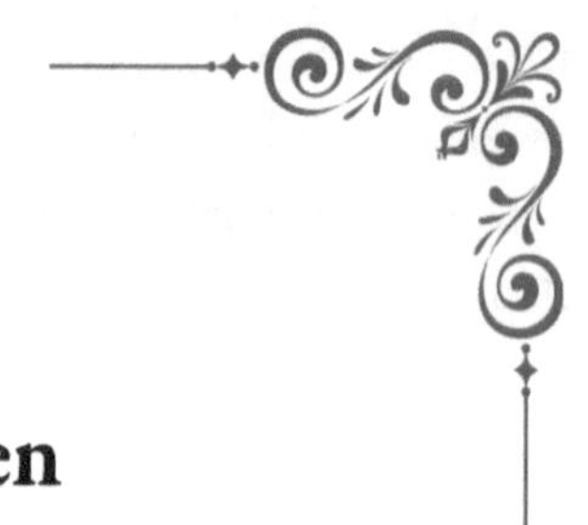

Chapter Eleven
The Colonial Attitude

Our whole society is being challenged to become aware of hidden and embedded ways which continue the old days of patriarchy and dominance of one group over another. There is resistance to this awareness, as exampled by the political rejection of critical race theory, which is an analysis of profound injustices that are factually present in our history. One may disagree with a given analysis from certain facts, but the resistance to even bringing up a factual awareness and attempting an analysis is telling. For a trait of the colonial and empire way is to shroud history, which would reveal its sins. It is also to continue the ways which are profitable and enable its way of life, no matter the harm or cost to others.

We all take part in varying degrees in the embedded injustices in our society, and it's hard to stop that because it is often more economical and more convenient. The real test of our principles is to what extent we sacrifice in order to maintain principles. If it withers away at the first indication of hardship, it is not very deeply held, or we have shielded ourselves from fully seeing or facing the realities of an injustice.

It was to my surprise that I find myself considering that experts in archaeology might also have an embedded colonial mentality. A deification of science which does not allow for the validity of other tools of exploration is an example. In exploring the meaning of a stone with markings, we might use our dreams, our artistic sensibility, our sense of resonance and feeling. All of this can be considered valid and as complimentary to the science.

A colonial attitude, however, is not open to such extensions. It would even remove Indigenous awareness and understanding of its own creations. If the Indigenous believe that Spirits can work on a stone and scientists believe this should not be considered, how is this disparity resolved? It would seem the first avenue to resolution would be a mutual respect to the varying modalities of study. An open discussion and forums could attempt to bridge these two worlds. But summary dismissal, a trait of empire mentality, which closes itself to any alternative worldview, is what is often encountered.

The colonial attitude does not need evidence, or to consider evidence outside of its perceived boundaries. It does not have or want the imaginative capacity to consider its vision is limited and that there are other viable ways to consider or view things. In a like way, we hold those who summarily dismiss scientific results, without considering the evidence, would be likewise be at fault.

In sum, we argue that there is no singular pontifical vision which embraces all reality. To make this mistake would be to the detriment of our own awareness and to the lives of others who have different views.

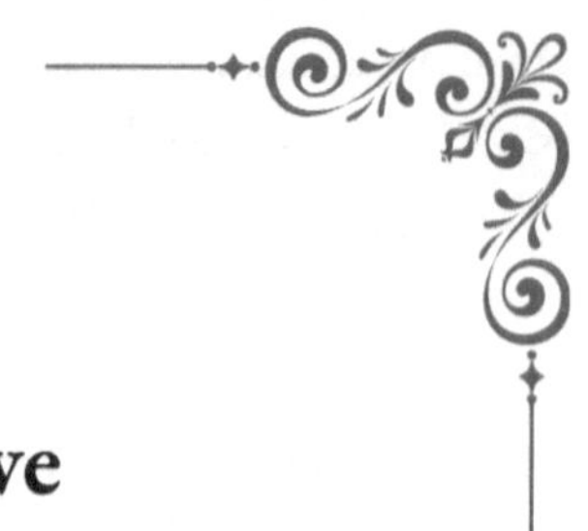

Chapter Twelve
Final Message: Let the Stone Speak

If we are not to let our study be distorted by a colonial attitude and be limited to the strictly scientific that limits the interaction of our being, we will allow the Stone to speak. But how does the Stone speak? We have already touched upon how the Stone's natural shape itself speaks to us through its beauty. We have found, too, that design elements present in the Stone's markings also speak to us. To hear something, to accurately perceive a message, we must see first see what is there. This involves spending time with the object, interacting in various ways, and being receptive to the reaction of our own deep being.

Perhaps each of us has such an object that calls us to mystery and brings a message to us. Perhaps we can share such objects with each other and see how their spiritual messages resonate with one another.

So, what is the message of this Stone with all its beauty and intricacy? If I had to summate all the work, I would say something like this: Respect and honor all the dimensions of the universe: the beauty of the earth, the beauty and gift of each other, and the beauty of the spiritual dimension, the *something more* from where we come and to where we go. The meaning of something is what it leads you to do. If your ideas lead you to hate others and not reach out in loving ways, it is not a good idea to live by. On the other hand, that which encourages our connection to one another with love, with the beauty and meaning in the universe, is a good idea to live by. Too much we have ghosted each other, instead of becoming enfleshed for one another. But the choice is ours and is made daily. The Stone invites you to take the side of beauty and love.

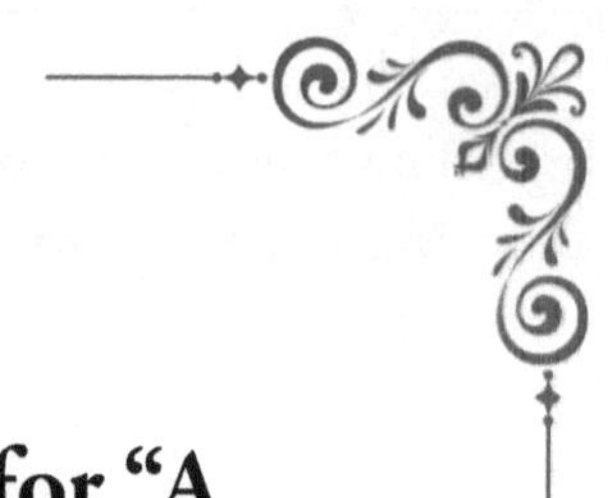

Appendix: Plates for "A Dozen Reasons Why"

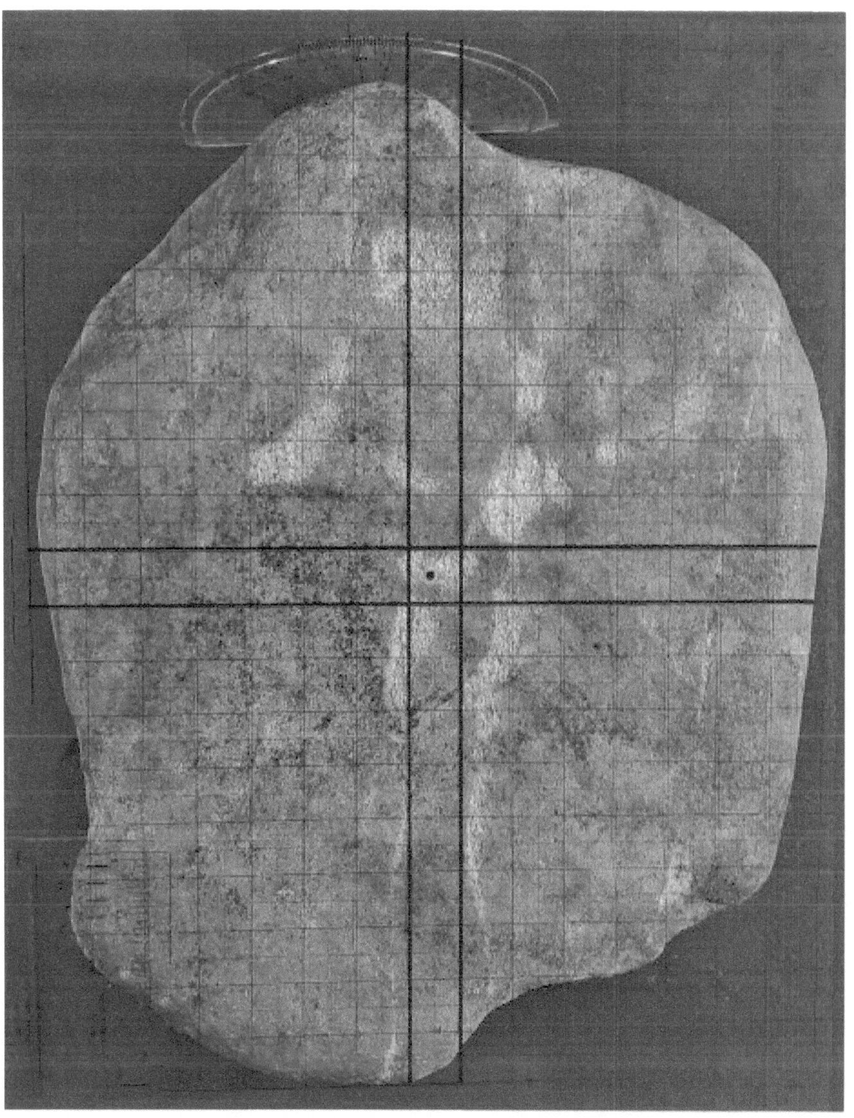

Plate 1: A Mark in the Center

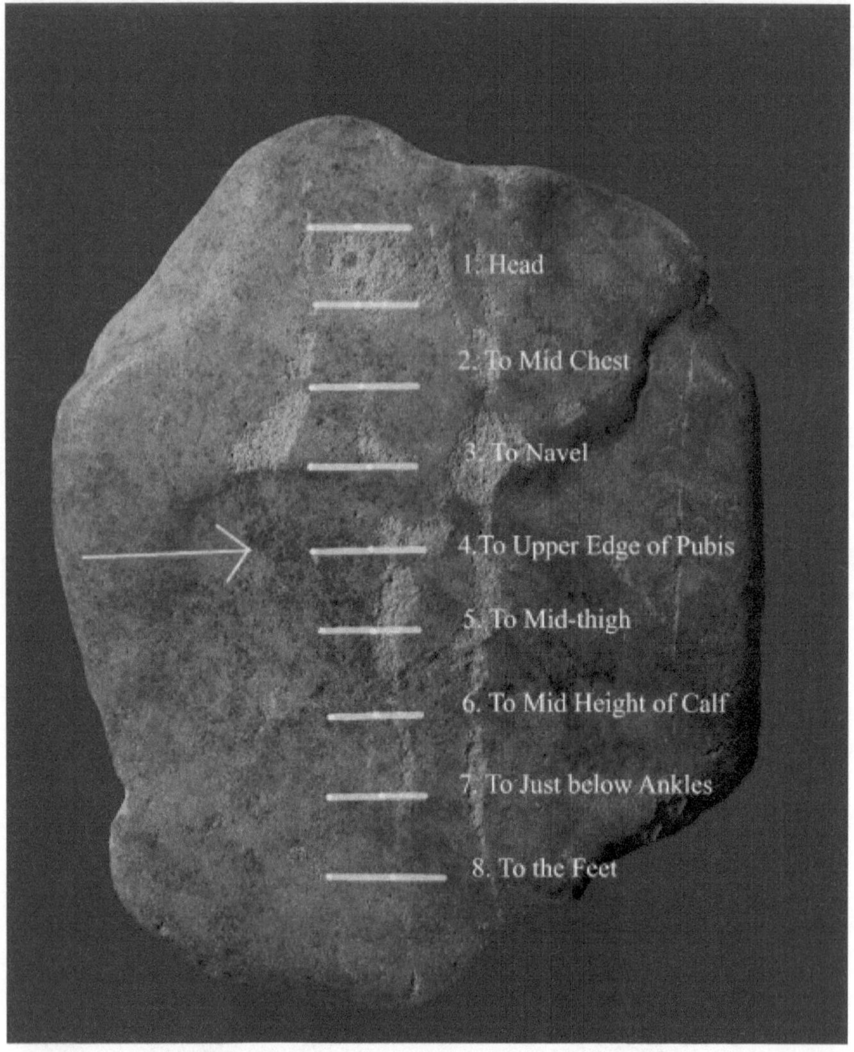

Plate 2: Anthropomorphic Proportions

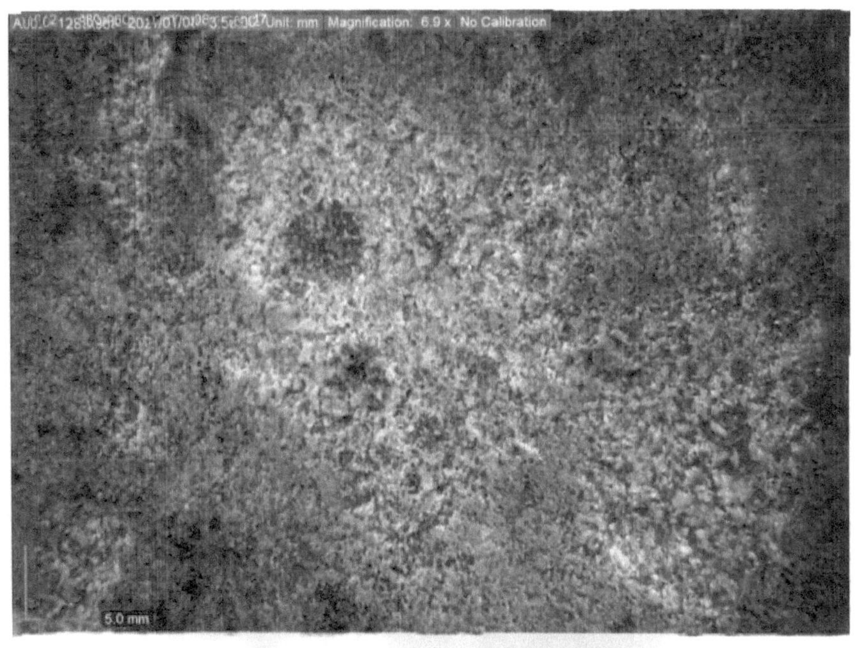

Plate 3: Heads with Facial Features

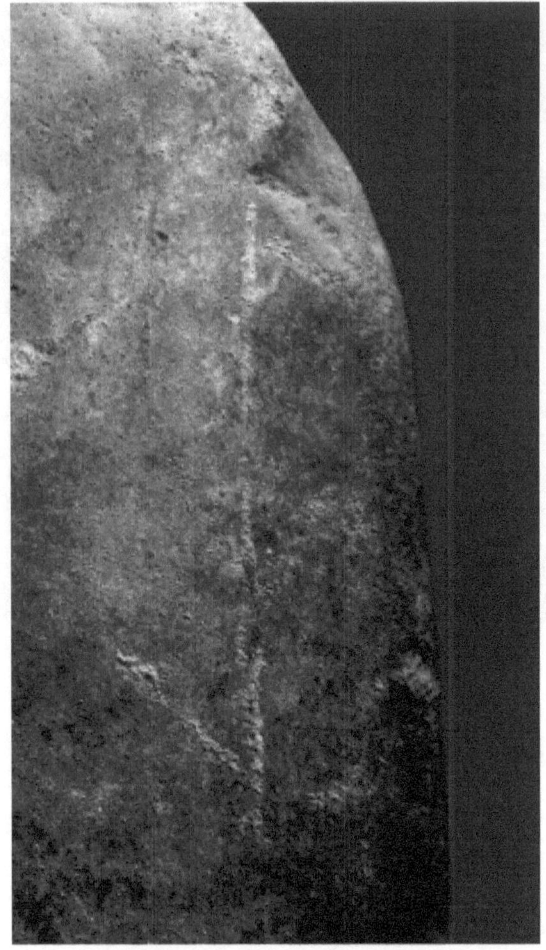

Plate 4: Plant-like Stalk with Design Elements
Processed with DStretch software

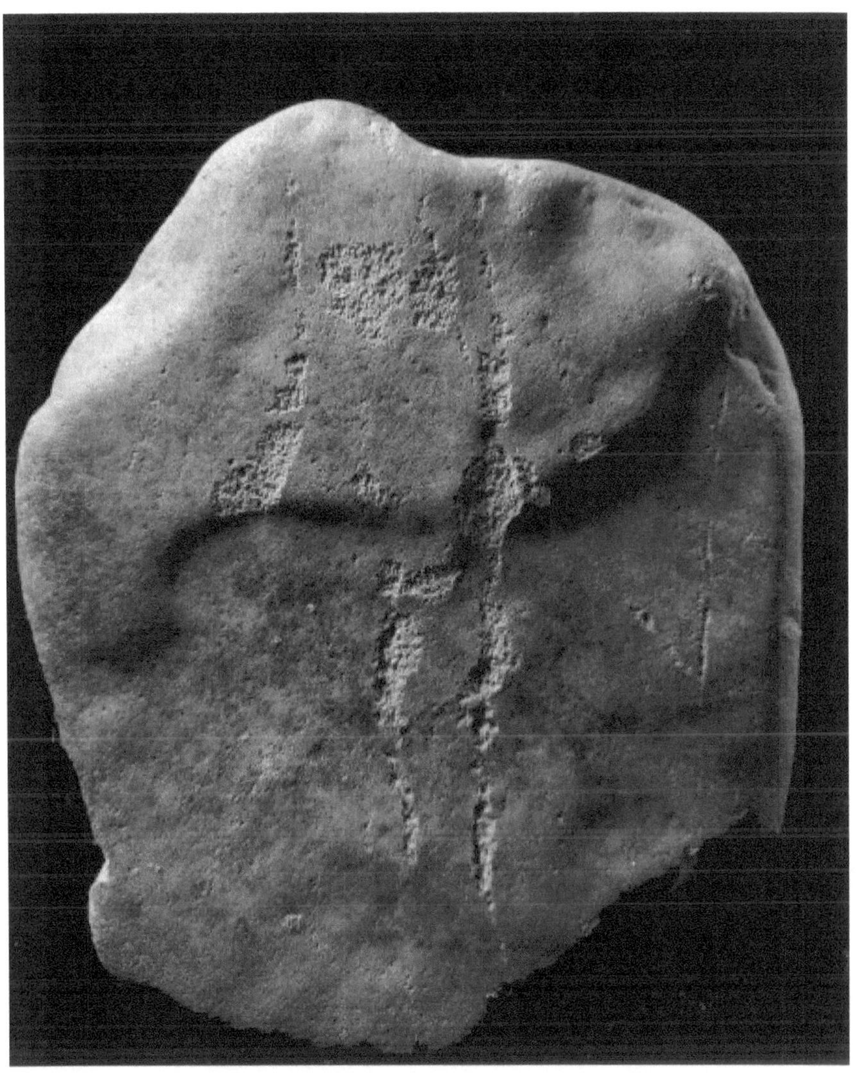

Plate 5: Sinuous Form with a Head

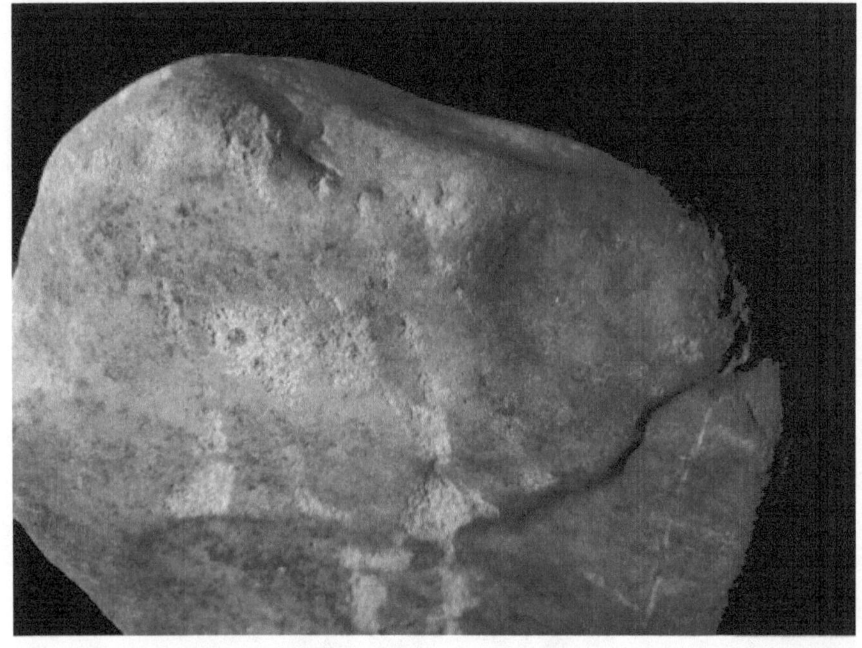

Plate 6: Quadruped Near the Stone's Top

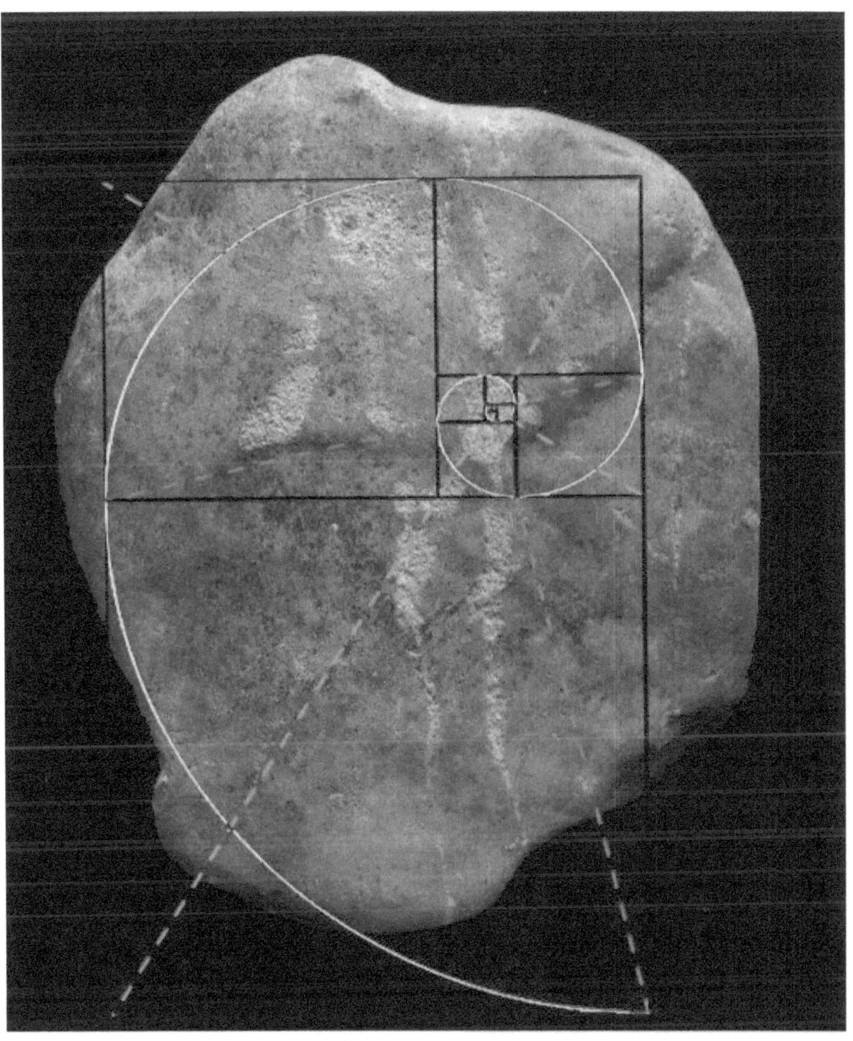

Plate 7: The Oval as a Center

MICHAEL A. SUSKO

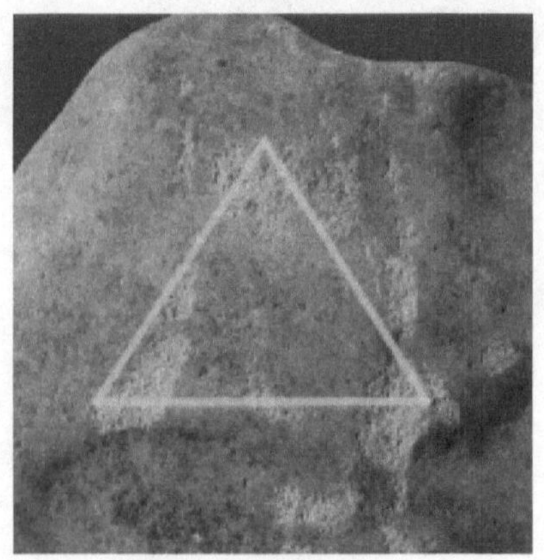

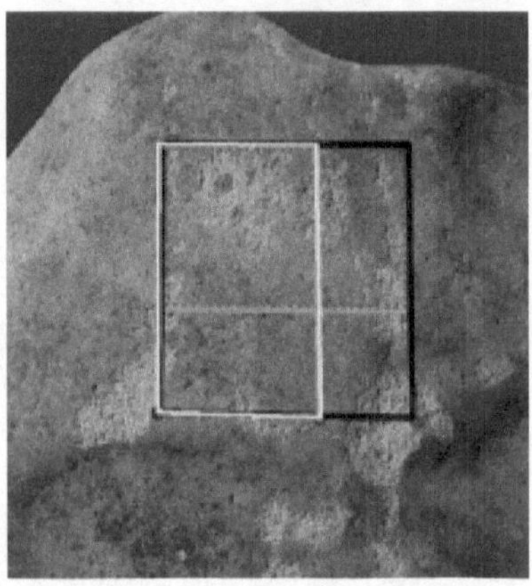

**Plates 8a and 8b: Equilateral Triangle and Golden Rectangles

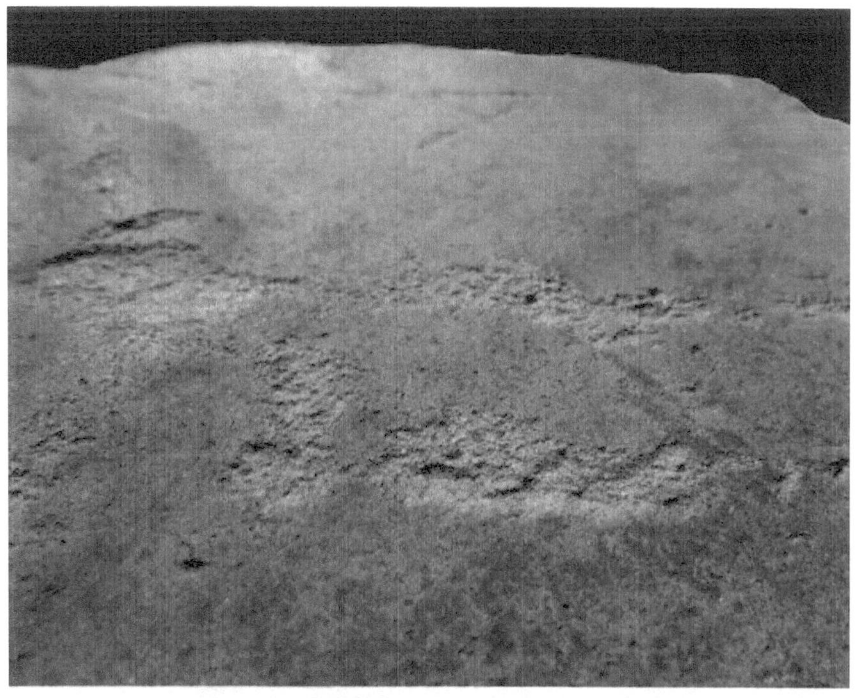

Plate 9: Dints and the Angle of Striking

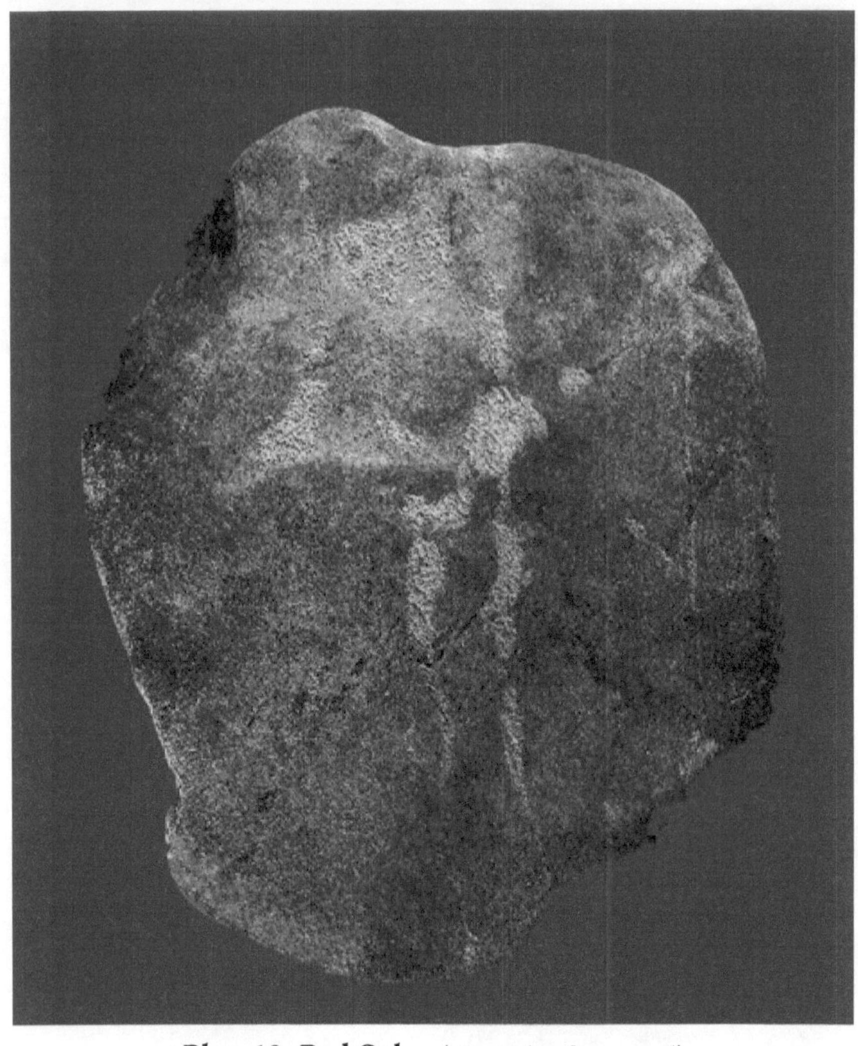

Plate 10: Red Ochre (DStretch software used)

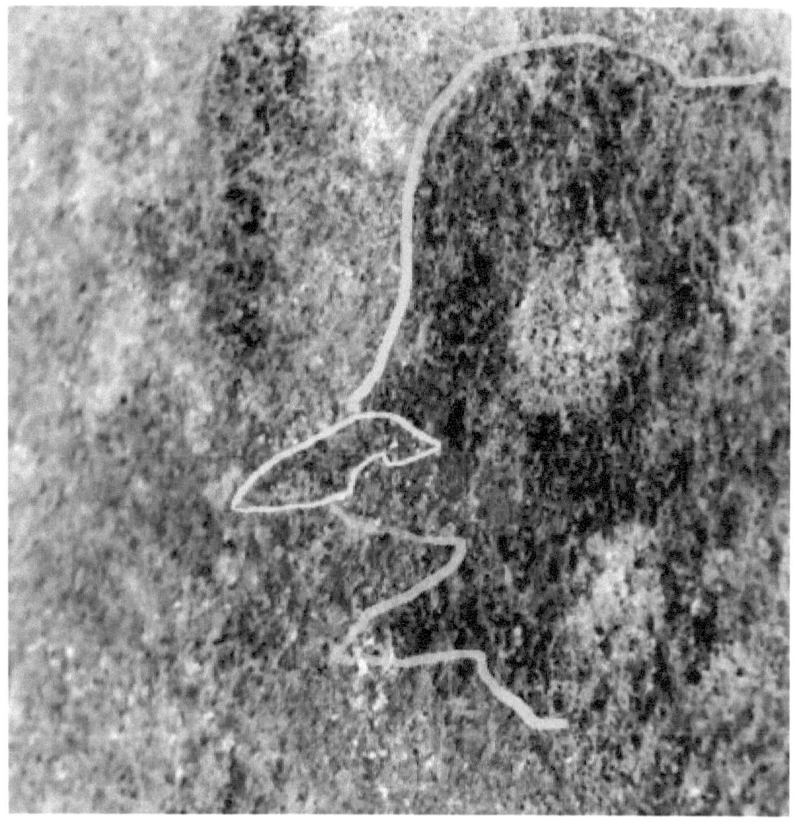

Plate 11: Beaked- Man
(Inverted, Processed by Photoshop)

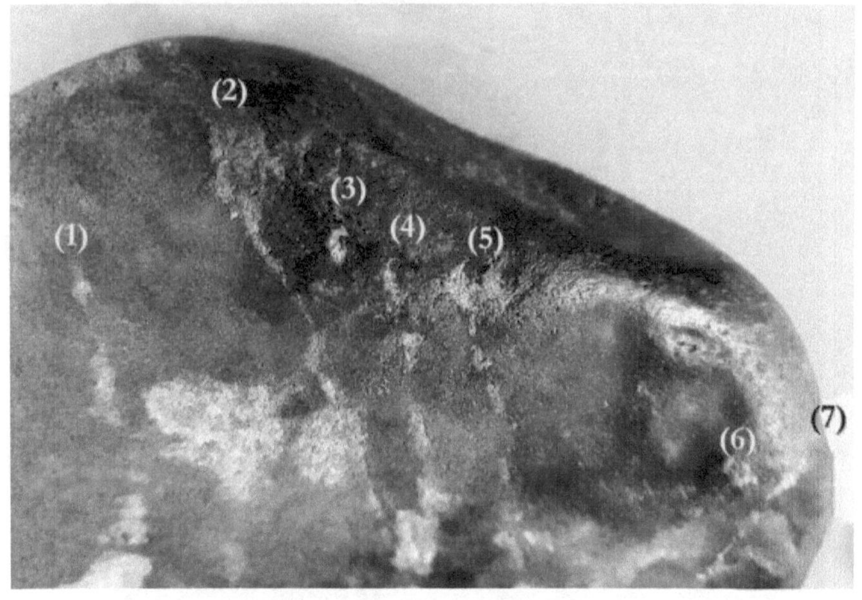

Plate 12: Designs at Top of Stone

Did you love *Philosopher Stone from the Lower Shenandoah*? Then you should read *Beyond the Portal: From Within the Mystery Stone*[1] by Michael A. Susko!

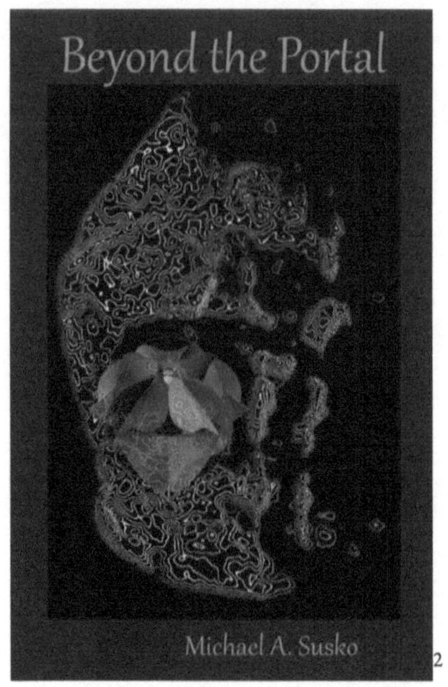

[2]

A hunter of mystery stones deciphers the markings of a petroglyph, which reveal an alternate view of the universe. A wide cast of beings appears, including a shamanic half-skeletal who serves as guide to this rich archetypal realm. The shapes on the Stone touch upon the twinned nature of reality, our hidden self, the nature of light/consciousness mixed with the demands of love, and the immortal nature of form. Come journey with us, following the continuing inspiration from the Mystery Stone from the Shenandoah.

Read more at https://www.allroneofus.com/.

---

1. https://books2read.com/u/md6L2W

2. https://books2read.com/u/md6L2W

Also by Michael A. Susko

Archetypal Worlds
Alwon in Another World: An Archetypal Voyage
Line On the Wall
The Alien's Gift
The Gold People
Spider Woman and the Timeroc
Quill Ears & the Other Earth
Darkwood and Dual with the Shadow Side
Giant Under the Mountain

Haikus and Photos
Flowers and Haikus
Haikus and Photos: Guatemalan Highlands
Haikus and Photos: Water Birds and Reflections
Haikus and Photos: Seasons of New River
Haikus and Photos: Yosemite Wilderness
Haikus and Photos: California Coast
Haikus and Photos: Canadian Rockies
Haikus and Photos: Hawaii's Exotic Landscapes
Haikus and Photos: Vienna, People with Buildings and Art
Haikus and Photos: Slovakian Castles and Hamlets
Haikus and Photos: Berlin, Light and Dark

Haikus and Photos: New Orleans, City of Immigrants
Haikus and Photos: Antietam Wind and Spirits
Haikus and Photos: Cosmogram from the Shenandoah
Haikus and Photos: Woodland Mystery Stone and World Archetypes
Haikus and Photos: Skeletal Human and Mississippian Art
Haikus and Photos: Mystery Stone's Animal Transformations
Photos and Haikus: Plant Mergings with Mystery Stone

Little Lion
The Lion and the Chameleon
The Elephant and the Chameleons

The Dreaming Series
Sleek Back
Streak and Cave Bear Dreaming
Moby and Marsupial Mole Dreaming

The Dream World Trilogy
Delphi, the Time Thief, and the Dream World
Detinna and the Cave God
The Resistance & the Empire

Worlds to the Side
Down Below and the Archon's Castle
Up Above and the Runaway
Across the Gulf and Journey Into Un-Time

On the Bay and a Child Found
In the Wild and Do One Wild Thing
On the Mountain and Two Are Missing
To the Beginning and Journey Through Here

Standalone
The Little People & the Time Riding XiXiShang
Animal Spell: A Gospel Story With an Evolutionary Twist
Child of the Elements
The Firekeeper
Transformational Stories: Voices for True Healing in Mental Health
Caseness and Narrative: Contrasting Approaches to People
Psychiatrically Labelled
Ten Pulses of Evolution & the Surprising Nature of Evolutionary Time
Street Images
Transformative Experiences, Psychiatric Research, and Informed
Consent
Street Images II
Up Above and Down Below
Life's Dynamic Vulnerability: A Paradigm Shift in Biology
Alien Ally
The Generation of LIfe: Imagery, Ritual and Experiences in Deep Caves
Twelve Suspects
2084: Clash of the Cults
Bats in the Future
Guard of the Dead
The Imagination Being
Mystery Stone from the Shenandoah
Beyond the Portal: From Within the Mystery Stone
Philosopher Stone from the Lower Shenandoah
The Mystery of Essence

Watch for more at https://www.allroneofus.com/.

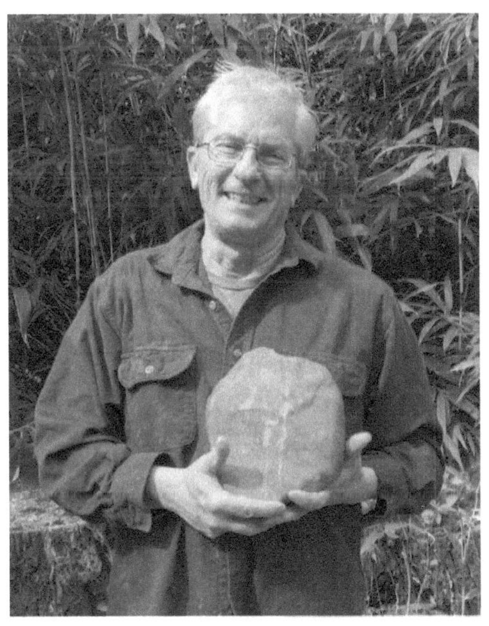

About the Author

The author, who majored in philosophy, taught a course for many years on the symbolism of Indigenous cultures. He has also made several trips to the interior of Guatemala, where he experienced the Indigenous lifestyle and ancient Mayan rituals. By sharing this work, the author hopes to return the gift that this Stone has given him.

Read more at https://www.allroneofus.com/.

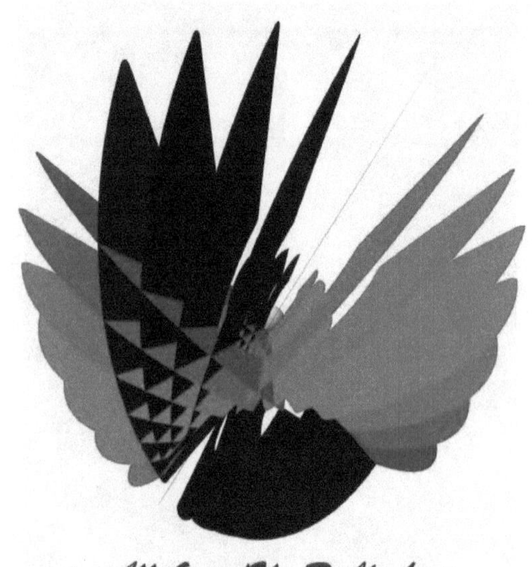

About the Publisher

AllrOneofUs Publishing seeks out work which will make a novel and qualitative addition to the world literature, and one that will last across generations. Many of these persons are in the later part of their life and have made exemplary contributions which are unrecognized. To cite a few examples, we recommend Rich Mullin's *Beyond Right and Wrong: Ethics as Nourishing the Good,* John Susko's *Flowers of the Night: Prose Poems from a Sentimental Friend,* and Dr. Curtis Adams' *Psychosis and the Humpty Dumpty Story.*